Larry Itliong

🖋 CHERRY LAKE PRESS

Published in the United States of America by Cherry Lake Publishing Group
Ann Arbor, Michigan
www.cherrylakepublishing.com

Reading Adviser: Beth Walker Gambro, MS, Ed., Reading Consultant, Yorkville, IL
Book Designer: Jennifer Wahi
Illustrator: Jeff Bane

Photo Credits: © R.M. Nunes/Shutterstock, 5; © Normand Fernandez/Shutterstock, 7, 22; © Busra Ispir/
Shutterstock, 9; © F Armstrong Photography/Shutterstock, 11; © Lucky Business/Shutterstock, 13;
© JessicaGirvan/Shutterstock, 15, 23; © Chat Karen Studio/Shutterstock, 17; © Lawrence Atienza/Shutterstock,
19; © Photo by Timothy Biley/flickr, 21; Jeff Bane, Cover, 1, 10, 12, 16; Various frames throughout,
Shutterstock images

Cherry Lake Press is an imprint of Cherry Lake Publishing Group.

Library of Congress Cataloging-in-Publication Data

Names: Loh-Hagan, Virginia, author. | Bane, Jeff, 1957- illustrator.
Title: Larry Itliong / by Virginia Loh-Hagan ; [illustrated by Jeff Bane].
Description: Ann Arbor, Michigan : Cherry Lake Publishing, [2022] | Series:
  My itty-bitty bio | Audience: Grades K-1
Identifiers: LCCN 2021036553 (print) | LCCN 2021036554 (ebook) | ISBN
  9781534198968 (hardcover) | ISBN 9781668900109 (paperback) | ISBN
  9781668905869 (ebook) | ISBN 9781668901540 (pdf)
Subjects: LCSH: Itliong, Larry, 1913-1977--Juvenile literature. | Labor
  leaders--United States--Biography--Juvenile literature. | Filipino
  American migrant agricultural laborers--Biography--Juvenile literature.
  | Filipino Americans--Biography--Juvenile literature.
Classification: LCC HD6509.I85 L64 2022 (print) | LCC HD6509.I85 (ebook)
  | DDC 331.88/13092 [B]--dc23
LC record available at https://lccn.loc.gov/2021036553
LC ebook record available at https://lccn.loc.gov/2021036554

Printed in the United States of America
Corporate Graphics

table of contents

About the author: When not writing, Dr. Virginia Loh-Hagan serves as the director of the Asian Pacific Islander Desi American (APIDA) Resource Center at San Diego State University. She identifies as Chinese American and is committed to amplifying APIDA communities. She lives in San Diego with her very tall husband and very naughty dogs.

About the illustrator: Jeff Bane and his two business partners own a studio along the American River in Folsom, California, home of the 1849 Gold Rush. When Jeff's not sketching or illustrating for clients, he's either swimming or kayaking in the river to relax.

I was born in 1913 in the Philippines.

I **immigrated** to the United States. I moved to California. I was 15 years old.

I wanted to be a **lawyer**. But I was poor. I could not go to school. I only completed the sixth grade.

What is your dream?

I had to work. I took any job. I worked on farms across the country. I noticed workers did not have rights. I wanted to change that. I formed **unions**.

There was a grape farm in Delano, California. Filipinos and Mexicans worked there. They were treated unfairly.

Have you ever been treated unfairly?

I led a **strike**. Filipino and Mexican Americans protested together.

15

The strike lasted 5 years. But it worked! Workers got paid more. They were treated better.

I also helped **retired** Filipino workers. I created a home for them.

I died in 1977. But my **legacy** lives on. I am known for protecting workers' rights.

What would you like to ask me?

1929

1910

Born
1913

1965

2010

↑
Died
1977

23

glossary

immigrated (IH-muh-gray-tuhd) moved permanently to another country

lawyer (LOY-uhr) a person whose job is to help people in matters relating to the law

legacy (LEH-guh-see) something handed down from one generation to another

retired (rih-TYE-uhrd) no longer working

strike (STRYK) a refusal to work as a form of protest

unions (YOON-yuhnz) groups of workers who organize to improve their working conditions

index